To go through a divorce and come out with money, sanity, and a bright future, please visit

TheMazerMethod.com

I dedicate this book to Dr. Howard Mazer.
Being your daughter gave me the confidence to overcome extreme adversity and the sense of humor needed to write this book. If all men were like my wonderful father, no woman would want to get divorced. I know that from wherever you are, that you're still watching me and cheering me on. I love and miss you more than words could ever express.

THE DIRTY SECRETS OF DIVORCE

Warning from a Licensed Psychologist who is a Diplomate of The American Board of Forensic Medicine:

"I deal with families that got destroyed by family court. The custody decisions are often horrific and make no sense. It is not unusual for the entire accrued wealth of the couple to be used up by this process. We are talking about hundreds of thousands of dollars. The courts will ask for a home study that will cost thousands of dollars. It will ask for a psychological analysis of each member of the family. It will mandate counseling. You can be assigned someone to reunify the family. In short, this is the beginning of a terrible situation that will last years. How do you avoid this? Read this book and follow its advice. Your future and the future of each member of your family depends on it."

This psychologist, who often testifies in court, prefers to remain anonymous for fear of retaliation.

TABLE OF CONTENTS

INTRODUCTION

Divorcing couples are lambs going to slaughter the moment one of them steps foot in a lawyer's office to start their divorce. They are Little Red Riding Hood at grandma's house. They are a fly speeding into a spider's web. They are Adam and Eve being handed an apple by a snake.

You get the point. And for that last one I should have made it plural, "snakes."

A trip through family court will plunder your assets. It is filled with conflicts of interest and practically no accountability.

So I say...

Don't be like Renee.

From family court, stay the frick away!

THAT PAPER THE SNAKE LAWYER IS HOLDING IS A RETAINER AGREEMENT.
"NO!" "DON'T SIGN!" "RUN, EVE, [ME AT THE BEGINNING OF MY DIVORCE] RUN!!"

FAMILY LAWYERS

There was a lawyer whose work on TV was praised.

On her desk was a hand with the middle finger raised.

"The Barracuda" was her infamous nickname...

So when she had a feeding frenzy on her clients assets,...

They had themselves to blame.

She cursed and screamed, and when I was her client...

I felt like I'd been tied up and whipped...

While at $525 per hour, my bank account was stripped.

Was she an anomaly?

No! According to Dutton's research on psychology,

Lawyers rank second,...

Right after CEOs in psychopathy.[2]

1: A RETAINER AGREEMENT IS A WORK FOR HIRE CONTRACT WHERE A CLIENT PAYS IN ADVANCE FOR WORK TO BE DONE.

2: KEVIN DUTTON IS THE AUTHOR OF THE BOOK, "THE WISDOM OF PSYCHOPATHS," AND A UNIVERSITY OF OXFORD PSYCHOLOGIST.

A LAWYER DIES AND GOES TO HEAVEN. WHEN HE GETS TO THE GATES
ST. PETER SAYS, "I SEE THAT YOU ARE 101 YEARS OLD."
THE ATTORNEY SAYS: "BUT I DIED BEFORE MY 60TH BIRTHDAY" TO WHICH ST. PETER REPLIED,
"WELL WE TOOK YOUR AGE FROM YOUR BILLING RECORDS..."

At hundreds of dollars per hour,...

Your attorney finds lots of work to do.

And don't kid yourself,...

Your ex is not the only person getting screwed.

The lawyers get your tax returns...

And know the value of your house.

When they turn your assets into legal fees...

Even if your ex Shtupped your best friend...

You'll hate them more than your ex- spouse.

The more trauma created,

the more cash made.

If you go to the family court route,

You won't have money for dates...

So you can forget about getting laid.

"RARE IS THE LEGAL BILL THAT DOES NOT INCLUDE AT LEAST SOME 'PADDING.' IN FACT, ACCORDING TO THE CALIFORNIA STATE BAR, MOST BILLS ARE INFLATED AT LEAST 10-30 PERCENT."

- HGExperts.com

"THE LEGAL FIELD ATTRACTS PSYCHOPATHS" is the title of an article by Debra Cassens Weis in the ABA (American Bar Association) Journal.

What comes first, the chicken or the rotten egg regarding the high rate of psychopathic lawyers? I'm with Debra Cassens Weis on this one. Here's why:

During the summer, while I was between years at Penn Law School, I rented an apartment with a few fellow law students. When I got there to move in, I found broken glass all over the floor in my room. The girl in my law school class who had broken the glass refused to clean it up. The other law students took her side and they all had a hissy fit together when I asked for help picking up the pieces. At the time I was shocked. Who acts like that? Now I'm so jaded from my years in family court, I wonder,
"WHAT LAWYER DOESN'T ACT LIKE THAT?"

When you can't afford college
so your kids drop out of school,
And your lawyer just got a Mercedes
and is building a pool,
You will feel like a fool.

So I say...
Don't be like Renee.
From lawyers, stay the frick away!

Why were my family lawyers so cranky, prone to angry outbursts, seemingly nuts, and unethical and sucky while I was paying them hundreds of dollars per hour? The following is only a partial explanation and it does not excuse them!

According to a John's Hopkins University study of more than 100 occupations, **"LAWYERS HAVE THE HIGHEST INCIDENCE OF DEPRESSION... IN 1996, LAWYERS BECAME THE PROFESSION WITH THE HIGHEST SUICIDE RATE... THE AMERICAN BAR ASSOCIATION ESTIMATES THAT 15 TO 20% OF ALL U.S. LAWYERS SUFFER FROM ALCOHOLISM AND SUBSTANCE ABUSE."**

- "The Depressed Lawyer", Psychology Today

Conforming to a study done by the ABA with the Hazeldon Betty Ford Foundation and reported in the New York Times in 2016, 1 in 3 practicing lawyers are problem drinkers. In the normal population, 6.8 percent of Americans over 18 had alcohol use disorders.

**""ANY WAY YOU LOOK AT IT, THIS DATA IS VERY ALARMING AND PAINTS A PICTURE OF AN UNSUSTAINABLE PROFESSIONAL CULTURE THAT'S HARMING TOO MANY PEOPLE,"
PATRICK R. KRILL[1] SAID"**

-"High Rate of Drinking Reported Among Lawyers," The New York Times

"DECADES OF RESEARCH HAS CONSISTENTLY REPORTED THE HIGHER PREVALENCE OF SUICIDE, ALCOHOL/DRUG ABUSE, DEPRESSION, STRESS, AND ANXIETY AMONG LAWYERS WHEN COMPARED TO OTHER PROFESSIONALS..."

-"Can We Finally Talk About The Elephant in the Room?" by Jeena Cho, Abovethelaw.com

---

1: "Patrick R. Krill is the co-author of the study and a lawyer who runs Hazeldon's substance-abuse treatment program for lawyers."
- Elizabeth olson, in the New York Times,"High Rate of Drinking Reported Among Lawyers

CUSTODY EVALUATORS

If you want to nurture your G-d complex...
While your clients kiss your ass.
If you secretly enjoy being a snake in the grass...

If your ego is big, and your scruples few...
Then custody evaluator is the profession for you!

My custody evaluator was a shmuck.
Whose interest in children was obviously the bucks.

At our custody evaluation meetings,...
My ex seemingly turned on the charm.
And in my high necked, A-line dresses,...
I looked and acted like an old schoolmarm.

The custody evaluators views...
On every topic were illogical and inane.
I smiled sweetly and nodded agreement...
As the neurons kept exploding in my brain.

ALLEGED, TYPICAL PARENT MEETING WITH A CUSTODY EVALUATOR

When he left voicemails, for each,

He charged approximately 50 dollars.

For that outrage, I could only keep smiling sweetly...

Pay it and not holler.

Turns out, he was nothing more than a shill.

I was shocked when I saw his approximately $20,000 bill.

For lots of reasons, chances are excellent that...

You too will get a shill.

And if your custody evaluator wants more business...

From your ex's Attorney...

He may declare you mentally ill.

Yes, with a lifetime of stability...

After you fill out a bubble form about your IQ and weight...

Being diagnosed as dangerous, bipolar and borderline...

Could be your fate.

But, it gets worse!

Have you ever wondered...

What your Mother-In-Law thinks of you?

You will find out as soon as...

Your custody evaluation is through.

"CUSTODY EVALUATIONS HAVE NO SCIENTIFIC EVIDENCE TO PROVE THEIR BENEFIT, YET LITIGANTS MAY FIND THEMSELVES COMPELLED TO PARTICIPATE IN THESE EVALUATIONS AT A SIGNIFICANT PRICE... THERE IS NO SCIENTIFIC EVIDENCE WHATSOEVER THAT A HIGHLY EXPERIENCED CUSTODY EVALUATOR PRODUCES A BETTER OUTCOME FOR CHILDREN THAN AN INEXPERIENCED EVALUATOR; THIS IS TRUE EVEN IF ONE WERE TO COMPARE A CUSTODY EVALUATOR TO A PIANO TEACHER OR A SEWER WORKER."

(or a monkey!)

- Ira Turkat PhD[1]

When it comes to custody evaluations, *"THERE ARE INFINITE SOURCES OF POTENTIAL BIAS...THE 'COMPELLING BODY OF RESEARCH' SHOWS... MANY CUSTODY EVALUATORS ARE UNABLE OR UNWILLING TO KEEP THEIR BIASES IN CHECK..."[HENCE, MONKEYS WOULD ACTUALLY MAKE BETTER CUSTODY RECOMMENDATIONS THAN PHDS, AND THEY'D ACCEPT PAYMENT IN BANANAS!]"...SINCE THE FAMILY LAW SYSTEM IS DESIGNED AS ADVERSARIAL (WIN/LOSE) IN NATURE, ATTORNEYS SPECIFICALLY SELECT CUSTODY EVALUATORS WHOSE KNOWN BIASES FAVOR THEIR PARTICULAR CLIENT."*

- Mark Baer Esq., HuffPost[2]

1: Dr. Ira Turkat's excerpt is from the American Journal of Family Law (Volume 32, Spring 2018) in the article "Psychologist Recommendations in custody Disputes Can be Harmful, Even Fatal"
2: Baer's, "If Utilizing A Custody Evaluation, Do So With Your Eyes Wide Open" was published in the huffpost in Jan. 7, 2018

All the lovely things your ex's friends and family...
Say about you will end up in a report.
A report that will be going to court.

My custody evaluator's notoriety for giving men favor...
Should have gotten me a fee waiver.

But, even if there was gender bias against me
Up the wazoo,
Evaluations made dads I know,
Bluer than blue too.

The lesson learned was...
If you want to maintain your sanity...
Save that gargantuan custody evaluation fee.

So I say...
Don't be like Renée.
From custody evaluators, stay the frick away!

CUSTODY EVALUATION SESSION:
DOESN'T THIS LOOK LIKE FUN? (NOT!)
WOULD YOU RATHER BUY A NEW CAR (OR KEEP YOUR HOUSE)
OR GO THROUGH THIS?

IN MANY JURISDICTIONS, THERE IS AN INTERMEDIARY LAYER OF THE JUDICIAL SYSTEM. LAWYERS ARE EMPLOYED BY COURT ADMINISTRATIVE UNITS TO MAKE LEGALLY-BINDING DETERMINATIONS IN SUPPORT AND CUSTODY ACTIONS. THESE MID-LEVEL JUDGES ARE CALLED MASTERS, HEARING OFFICERS, MAGISTRATES, AND STATE'S ATTORNEYS.

When you go to court you lose control.

You have stepped into the rabbit hole.

A whole cast of characters awaits you.

You'll be lucky if you still have a house, and kids...

When they're through.

Your hearings might be held in front of Masters.

My experiences with those guys were a total disaster.

Masters used to abuse slaves and Genies.

Now, they abuse parents and are total weenies, allegedly...

At my Equitable Distribution (ED)[1] hearing...

The Master in what sure looks like a kickback scheme...

With a Realtor threatened me into a settlement...

Which I think was a massive crime.

My friends who were bedridden after their ED hearings...

Claim their Masters were as bad as mine.

1: EQUITABLE DISTRIBUTION IS THE DIVIDING OF MARITAL ASSESTS USED BY COURTS DURING DIVORCE PROCEEDINGS.

"THE CHILDREN THEMSELVES ARE ALWAYS USED LIKE A PAWN..."
- Dr. Drew Pinsky on Bloomberg Television

Custody is only one type of threat apparently used to force divorcing people into disastrous settlements. Among other extreme financial threats, the Master also told me that if I didn't sign the nightmare settlement, she'd give my ex my intellectual property rights even on projects started after my divorce! For a better understanding of this cartoon, and of how and why some Masters are allegedly using ED to steal property, go to page 21.

One of my ex's attorneys had been...
A Master in the court for years.
How lucky for my ex! She was arguing our cases in front of...
Her former co-workers, her good friends, and peers.

I filed for a change of venue.
But, the Judge denied me that...
Even though my ex's lawyer's reputation...
For backroom deals was seemingly making her wallet fat.

I saw my ex's attorney and the custody Master together...
Outside of court.
I wonder if ex-parte communication with a Master is a tort.

Were the Masters and lawyers racketeering?
Are they part of a mob?
Was my ex's attorney giving the custody Master...
Some type of job? (LOL)

You wouldn't leave decisions...
About your money, house, and kids to the average Joe.
If you give those decisions to Masters, you are a schmo.

So I say...
Don't be like Renée.
From Masters, stay the frick away!

1: Ex-parte means from one party, one sided.
2: A tort is a wrongful act for which the injured party can bring a civil lawsuit.

DIVORCE IS LISTED FIRST UNDER "COMMON REASONS FOR FORECLOSURE"
on the University of Illinois Extension, the University of Illinois at Urbana-Champaign,
College of ACES website, and adopted from the National Association of Foreclosure Prevention Professionals.

WHAT'S THE DEAL WITH THE MARITAL HOMES AND THE MASTERS? KICK BACKS? MAKING MONEY OFF FORECLOSURES AND SHERIFF SALES? HERE IS SOME INSIGHT.

Upon facts and information given to me by other Realtors, the alleged scam I dealt with was the following. In exchange for getting a dream financial settlement, my ex in an alleged backroom deal likely promised to force me to use the Realtor named in the Settlement Agreement I was threatened into signing. That Realtor would sell our marital home cheap to a developer who would renovate it and sell the newly developed home for even bigger money. The Realtor would then get another commission from the second sale and the Master would allegedly get her kickback. I put a monkey wrench in that alleged scheme. My ED Master is no longer a Master in that courthouse and I hear the Realtor went bankrupt. I have a feeling I had something to do with those things, but, my kids and I were still gravely harmed by that alleged scam and the family court players are still seemingly up to their dirty tricks.

My Master's replacement allegedly pulled a similar scam on my close friend Maureen.

After being threatened into signing a grossly unfair Settlement Agreement, she wrote the following in a complaint to the President Judge, "I believed that I was going to trial for a divorce that was not reaching a settlement... Instead what I experienced was a sham and a farce... I completely feel that my property was taken under the threat of a more punitive outcome...I do not know where you may have found Master.....Was it in the land of Oz, waiting for a heart?" (Love you, Maureen!) In her case, I believe the motivation for the fraud was family court players trying to profit from getting a lien on her marital home.

Was Maureen correct about threats of more punitive outcomes for going to trial? My case seems to answer that question in the affirmative. The Master allegedly threatened me that if I went to trial, I'd lose an asset. I started the trial anyway. The Master then stopped the trial to allegedly threaten me with things so scary I felt I had no choice, but to sign the grossly unfair settlement agreement. It was made clear to me that for daring to start the trial, however, that asset was taken away from me in the settlement agreement.

Armin, another wonderful woman with a different Master in our same court wrote to the press, "I was forced to short sale my house when I had the means to keep it. The scam is also with the real estate agents. Mine was horrible!" Her ex had one of the same attorneys as mine; the one who used to be a Master in the court. About her experience, Armin added, "Are these people above law and God? Why can't someone stop them for God's sake?"

To accomplish these travesties, the Master allegedly first needs to make sure you get hardly any assets in those unfair Settlement Agreements so they can force the house sales. Hence, divorcing victims typically lose way more than just their house.

In a different county, an Ivy League educated woman, who is now back living with her mother in her sixties because of family court shenanigans, complained to her county commissioners about asset stripping and marital home foreclosures caused by family court. She argued, "I don't believe that you can run this county without stealing the personal assets of families... My ex-husband was stunned by what they did to us. Everything we worked for our entire life was stolen. It is not just this county, but the family court across Pennsylvania."

The response to these complaints... Crickets.

It is not just Pennsylvania. There are formerly financially stable people all over America who are now broke and homeless because of alleged family court scams. STAY AWAY!!!

JUDGES

Judges rule with impunity...

Because they have immunity.

I could talk about Stump v. Sparkman...

And use lots of legalese.

But, all you really need to know is that...

Judges have immunity, so...

They can do pretty much whatever the hell they please.

Can Judges be malicious?

Can they be corruptly pernicious?

Can they ignore the Constitution?

Can they turn your life into a mess?

You can't sue Judges for judicial acts...

So the answer to those questions seems to be yes.

Should Judges be given such latitude?

Are they superior humans with tremendous aptitude?

What was Porngate? *"FAT JOKES. GAY JOKES. RACIST JOKES. DOMESTIC-VIOLENCE JOKES. THE BULK OF WHICH WERE SENT ON STATE COMPUTERS, ON STATE TIME, FROM ONE STATE EMPLOYEE TO ANOTHER... THE EMAILS WERE LIKE STRANDS OF A SPIDERWEB, STRETCHING OUT IN EVERY POSSIBLE DIRECTION, CONNECTING SMALL-TOWN ATTORNEYS TO BIG-NAME PROSECUTORS TO STATE SUPREME COURT JUSTICES... ONE PHOTO COLLECTION TITLED "BLONDE BANANA SPLIT" CONTAINED MORE THAN 30 IMAGES OF TWO WOMEN STUFFING BANANAS INSIDE EACH OTHER'S EVERY HOLE... THE MEN—THEY WERE ALMOST ALL MEN—EXCHANGING THESE IMAGES WERE AMONG THE MOST PROMINENT NAMES IN THE STATE'S JUDICIAL SYSTEM."*

\- David Gamacorta, Esquire Magazine[1]

JUDGES *"ARE NOT LIABLE TO CIVIL ACTIONS FOR THEIR JUDICIAL ACTS, EVEN WHEN SUCH ACTS...ARE ALLEGED TO HAVE BEEN DONE MALICIOUSLY OR CORRUPTLY."*

\- Bradley v. Fisher[2]

"A JUDGE WILL NOT BE DEPRIVED OF IMMUNITY BECAUSE THE ACTION HE TOOK WAS IN ERROR WAS DONE MALICIOUSLY OR WAS IN EXCESS OF HIS AUTHORITY"

\- Stump v. Sparkman[3]

"IF YOU GIVE PEOPLE POWER WITHOUT OVERSIGHT, IT'S A PRESCRIPTION FOR ABUSE."

-Dr. Philip Zimbardo in his ted talk[4]

"AS MOST CALIFORNIANS WHO HAVE BEEN FORCED TO DEAL WITH THE CALIFORNIA COURTS HAVE LEARNED, THE RULE OF LAW HAS BEEN SUPPLANTED BY THE AVARICE OF JUDGES. TALK WITH SOMEONE WHO HAS BEEN IN FAMILY COURT. THE STORIES ARE UNBELIEVABLE, BUT MOST LIKELY CORRECT. CHILDREN ARE ABUSED AND ESSENTIALLY HELD FOR RANSOM WHILE PARENTS HAVE TO UNDERGO PSYCHOLOGICAL COUNSELING FOR "DUAL DIAGNOSES." SURPRISE, SURPRISE, THE PSYCHOLOGIST IS A FRIEND OF THE JUDGE. AS HUFF POST REPORTED IN 2017, JUDGES MAKE AWARDS IN FAVOR OF THE UN-FIT PARENT KNOWING THAT THE FIT PARENTS WILL SPEND LARGE SUMS OF MONEY TO PROTECT THE CHILDREN. JUDICIAL IMMUNITY HAS PROVEN TO BE A TOTAL FAILURE."

\- Richard Lee Abrams in City Watch Los Angeles[5]

1: David Gamacorta published, "The Great Pennsylvania Government Porn Caper," in esquire magazine on Feb. 24, 2016
2: Bradley v. Fisher, 80 U.S. (13 Wall.) 335 (1871), U.S. Supreme Court Decision
3: Stump v. Sparkman, 435 U.S. 349 (1978), U.S. Supreme Court Decision
4: "The Psychology of Evil." Philip Zimbardo is a psychologist and Professor Emeritus at Stanford University
5: Richard Lee Abrams wrote "How Corrupt Judges Are Destroying Our Society" Which was Published in City Watch Los Angeles

Supreme Court Judges in Pennsylvania...

Were caught sending porn.

In that scandal known as Porngate,...

I've heard that with bananas women were adorned.

A Reuters investigation found...

That in Chambers a Judge fooled around.

And oaths and laws thousands of Judges broke.*

If you think Judges are superior,...

I want to know what you smoke?!

How do these men in robes get selected?

In most states, they are elected.

Judges get campaign money from lawyers who are rich.

Studies show campaign contributions influence decisions.

Your Judge could be your ex's attorney's bitch.

When the Judge's Orders look like...

They are coming out of the Third Reich.

When those reviewing your case in horror scream,

"Yikes!"

"Montana Judiciary Caught Lobbying Against Judicial Accountability in Email Scandal" Title of a January 4, 2022 article by Megan Fox in PJ Media.

If you think you will get justice by...

Filing appeals and ethics complaints...

That is so cute!

I find your naivety quaint.

If you do those things, you're barking up the wrong tree.

Expect retaliation, like a contempt[1] finding...

And the Judge making you pay your ex's attorney fees.

I know of cases where Judges had...

Moms and Dads sleeping on prison cots.

And "gag" ordered so against judicial abuses...

The parents couldn't do squat.

And when you start to actually gag...

Because your Judge's behavior is abominable...

You still have to call that piece of dog doo doo,...

"The Honorable."

So I say...

Don't be like Renee.

From Judges, stay the frick away!

1: CONTEMPT OF COURT IS THE OFFENSE OF DISOBEDIENCE TOWARD OR INTERFERENCE WITH THE JUDICIARY.

"OVER THE PAST TWO DECADES, MORE THAN 1,000 ETHICS COMPLAINTS HAVE BEEN LODGED AGAINST SOUTH CAROLINA JUDGES WHO HANDLE THE STATE'S MAJOR CASES IN CIRCUIT COURT. BEYOND MERE COURTROOM DISPUTES, THE COMPLAINTS CONTAIN SERIOUS CONCERNS ABOUT ABUSE OF OFFICE, INCLUDING ALLEGATIONS OF INFLUENCE PEDDLING OR JUDGES MISHANDLING CONFLICTS OF INTEREST. THE NUMBER OF JUDGES PUNISHED PUBLICLY AS A RESULT: ZERO."

- Joseph Craney, "South Carolina: The State Where Judges Rule Themselves in Secret," in ProPublica

According to Adam Liptak in a New York Times article, **"ANY NUMBER OF STUDIES HAVE FOUND THAT ELECTIONS CAN AFFECT JUDICIAL BEHAVIOR."**

The Judicial Conduct Board

You after a few months in family court

"ONLY THREE STATES SCORE HIGHER THAN D+ IN STATE INTEGRITY INVESTIGATION; 11 FLUNK...MORE OFTEN THAN NOT, THE STATE INTEGRITY INVESTIGATION SHOWS, THOSE ENTITIES (THAT POLICE ETHICS LAWS) ARE UNDERFUNDED, SUBJECT TO POLITICAL INTERFERENCE OR ARE SIMPLY UNABLE OR UNWILLING TO INITIATE INVESTIGATIONS OR IMPOSE SANCTIONS."

- Nicholas Kusnetz[1]

In that Investigation Pennsylvania got an F and one of the reasons was the absence of effective ethics entities. Philadelphia, "city of brotherly love," my ass. Pennsylvania, where the constitution was written and is now ignored. Ben Franklin must be rolling around in his grave!

1: Nicholas Kusnetz on the website of the Pulitzer Prize-Winning, The Center for Public Integrity who partnered with Global Integrity on this investigation.

COURT APPOINTEES

When your divorce has made you broke...

And your custody schedule is a cruel joke...

Are you feeling down?

Then it's time for family court to bring in the clowns.

For your troubles family court has a fix.

One that looks a lot like a profit-making trick.

The Judge Orders the use of GALs[1], Parent Coordinators[2],

Co-parenting counselors, and all sorts of court appointees.

And, even if you don't want them,...

Your Judge's Orders might say you agreed.

These Court Ordered lawyers and therapists...

Come with Machiavellian twists.

1: GAL (GUARDIAN AD LITEM)- IN FAMILY COURT AN APPOINTED LAWYER WHO MAKES CHILD CUSTODY AND PARENT-TIME RECOMMENDATIONS TO THE COURT
2: PARENT COORDINATORS ARE COURT-ORDERED, HIGH PAID REFEREES WHO INTERFERE IN PARENTING DECISIONS WHEN PARENTS CANNOT AGREE

COURT-ORDERED PSYCHIATRIC EVALUATION OF A TYPICAL MOTHER.

Court appointees rack up billable hours...
As quickly as bees pollinate flowers.

For these folks, you are forced to pay, and pay, and pay...
They decide how often you see them...
And there seems to be nothing you can do...
To make them go away.

Plus, who you use...
You often don't get to choose.

The Judge can get your court appointee evaluations1...
And session notes turning your HIPAA rights to toast.
Kiss your court appointee's ass or this is another way...
You could get wrongly mentally ill diagnosed.

On your kid's new Step-Mom or Dad...
Are you busy conjuring up a hex?
Then, it might be time for forced super-expensive...
Co-parenting counseling with that nightmare and your ex.

1: This is referring to the psychological evaluations, done by court appointed mental health professionals, that the judge can force you to get.

"THERE IS NO DEFINITION OF A MENTAL DISORDER. IT'S BULLSHIT. I MEAN, YOU JUST CAN'T DEFINE IT." MENTAL HEALTH PROFESSIONALS ARE "MAKING DISEASES OUT OF EVERYDAY SUFFERING..."

-Allen Francis[1]

"FROM JUDGES, PSYCHOLOGISTS, LAWYERS FOR THE CHILDREN, GUARDIANS-AD-LITEM, AND MENTAL HEALTH APPOINTEES WHO SERVE AS PARENTING COORDINATORS, PARENTING COACHES, SPECIAL MASTERS, REUNIFICATION COUNSELORS, EXPERT WITNESSES AND MEDIATORS... THE FAMILY LAW COTTAGE INDUSTRY HAS EXPLODED INTO A HIGHLY PROFITABLE, AND FOR THE MOST PART, COMPLETELY UNREGULATED, PROFIT-DRIVEN INDUSTRY THAT CHARGES EXORBITANT FEES TO PARENTS FOR SERVICES THEY DO NOT WANT OR NEED, WHILE FAR TOO MANY CHILDREN SUFFER BY BEING FORCED BY COURT ORDER TO LIVE OR VISIT A PARENT IN A VIOLENT OR ABUSIVE HOME."

- From https://centerforjudicialexcellence.org/

"...IN THE CASE OF FAMILY AND MATRIMONIAL COURT PSYCHOLOGISTS, OPD'S (OFFICE OF PROFESSIONAL DISCIPLINE THAT OVERSEES PSYCHOLOGISTS IN NEW YORK) OVERSIGHT IS NOT SO MUCH FLAWED AS IT IS ABSENT ENTIRELY."

- Joaquin Sapien, ProPublica[2]

1: Allen Francis is the "lead editor of the fourth edition of the American Association's Diagnostic and Statistical Manual of Mental Disorders." (The DSM - IV) in Inside, The Battle To Define Mental Illness by Gary Greenberg in WIRED.

2: The ProPublica article, "For New York Families in Custody Fights, a 'Black Hole' of Oversight" was written by Joaquin Sapien

Against my strong objections, my Judge averred...
I agreed to co-parenting counseling with my ex...
And my replacement with whom he had a baby...
So he must have been having sex.

Are you wondering, "How did that torture therapy go?"
The court ordered psychologist made lots of dough.

Do you want a court-appointed lawyer charging lawyer fees...
To decide you can't take your kid for a hair cut?
If you do, you're a nut.

So I say...
Don't be like Renee.
From court appointees, stay the frick away!

A lawsuit in Missouri alleges a scheme whereby, "At the end of the court process, parents are broke and kids are traumatized while GALs, Court-Appointed psychologists and therapists are enriched." In my humble opinion, based on overwhelming evidence, court players colluding to make exorbitant profits off your custody case, is going on all over the country.

Megan Fox, PJ Media (pjmedia.com), March 2, 2021, "31 Missouri Judges Recuse Themselves from Lawsuit Alleging Family Court Guardians and Psychologists Orchestrated Money-Making Scheme"

REVELATION!!!
PEOPLE DEALING WITH THE TRAVESTIES GOING ON IN FAMILY COURTS ARE SUFFERING. THEN THEY GET COURT-ORDERED INTO PSYCHIATRIC EVALUATIONS. THE COURT APPOINTEES DOING THOSE EVALUATIONS SEEMINGLY HAVE CONFLICTS OF INTEREST GALORE! THAT IS A RECIPE FOR GETTING PARENTS LABELED WITH BOGUS "MENTAL ILLNESS" DIAGNOSIS. AS THE SAGE SPIRITUAL ADVISOR MARIANNE WILLIAMSON EXPLAINED ON HBO'S REAL TIME WITH BILL MAHER, WHEN TALKING ABOUT SEVERE DISAPPOINTMENTS LIKE DIVORCE, "NORMAL HUMAN DESPAIR", IS "NOT A MENTAL ILLNESS." I SAY, AMEN! MAKE THAT WOMAN A COURT APPOINTEE!

ALLEGED TYPICAL PARENT COORDINATION SESSION... KISS YOUR PARENT
COORDINATOR'S ASS OR YOUR RELATIONSHIP WITH YOUR KIDS WON'T LAST

"A DIVORCE OR CUSTODY BATTLE WILL EASILY PUT ANYBODY MAKING UNDER $100,000 PER YEAR INTO A BANKRUPTCY."

-Attorney James O. Wyre II[1]

"THE PROBLEM WITH FAMILY COURT IS THAT FINANCIAL INTERESTS OUTWEIGH THE JUDICIAL ISSUES, AND THE ENTIRE LEGAL SYSTEM HAS BEEN GEARED TO SUPPORT THE FINANCIAL PLUNDER OF CLIENTS."

-Keith Harmon Snow[2]

"WHILE EACH OF THESE CASES EXAMINED IN ISOLATION WOULD SEEM UNBELIEVABLE, TAKEN TOGETHER THEY FORM AN INESCAPABLE PORTRAYAL OF A NATIONAL TREND OF CRUELTY AND CORRUPTION ON THE PART OF CUSTODY COURTS."

-Patrice Lenowitz and Lundy Bancroft, "Forbidden to Protect"[3]

"MOST PEOPLE ATTRACTED TO POWER ARE AT BEST MEDIOCRE AND USUALLY VENAL..." THE QUESTION IS NOT HOW TO GET GOOD PEOPLE TO RULE; THE QUESTION IS: HOW TO STOP THE POWERFUL FROM DOING AS MUCH DAMAGE AS THEY CAN TO US.

- Karl Popper, Generally Regarded as one of the 20th century's greatest philosophers of science[4] and emphasized by pulitzer prize winning journalist, Chris Hedges.

The answer to Popper and Hedges' question - How do we stop the powerful from damaging us?

STAY OUT OF FAMILY COURT!!!

1: Attorney James O. Wyre II, Bankruptcy Professional Center, Inc. Comway Arkansas
2:Keith Harmon Snow is an award-winning journalist, the excerpt is from the book ,"Worst Interests of the Child"
3: From the Playbill for "Forbidden to Protect," an original play by Patrice Lenowitz founder of the "Nurtured Parent" and Best Selling Author Lundy Bancroft. That play uses actual stories to expose the systemic human rights Violations committed by custody courts.
4: Sir Karl Raimund Popper CH FBA FRS was an Austrian born philosopher and professor

SO WHAT DO YOU DO...

When your spouse is so very, very bad, your car mechanic or kid's Sunday school teacher starts looking really, really good?

Having been through family court, I can unequivocally say that given this hypothetical scenario, I would choose a psychopathic, child torturing spouse I haven't had sex with in years over child torturing psychopathic lawyers and Judges who screw me on a daily basis.

Especially if that spouse helps pay the mortgage! But, there are other options. If you want to get divorced, but think going broke and dealing with greed driven miscreants while getting diagnosed mentally ill isn't for you, check out the alternatives I've highlighted on the next pages.*

Then figure out which one (or combination of them) is right for your situation and do everything in your power to stay the frick away from family court.

---

* While reading about these alternatives in this book, keep in mind that the information in this book is provided for informational purposes only and is not legal advice nor should it be taken or construed as legal advice. The author and publisher assumes no liability for the use or interpretation of any information contained in this book. The information in this book is intended, but not guaranteed or promised, to be complete, correct or up-to-date. Moreover, when commenting on these alternatives, the author is merely giving her opinions. Throughout the entire book, the author is merely giving her opinions. The author recommends that regarding all the topics included in this book, you do your own research.

1. RESTRUCTURE YOUR MARRIAGE WITH INFORMAL ARRANGEMENTS

That could include:

A.   Living separate lives while sharing the house and kids: You may already be doing this, but communicating and laying out the specifics of your informal arrangement, could be healthier and happier than cheating and pretending everything is honky dory. This arrangement will work best if you like each other as friends and roommates but would rather clean the garage than visit your in-laws. For this arrangement to succeed, details will need to be worked out. For example, if your separate life includes swinger's parties, can you have them at your house? LOL!

B.   Platonic Marriage: While lots of marriages become platonic over time, under this option, turning the marriage celibate would be a mutually agreed upon arrangement. As any evolutionary biologist will tell you, lust fades. But, a desire to keep your assets and kids does not! This arrangement will work best if you like each other as friends and roommates but would rather clean the garage than have sex with each other.

For this arrangement to succeed, details will need to be worked out. For example, does the celibacy only apply to your marriage? If not, are mutual friends and in-laws off limits? LOL!

C.   Informal Separation: One partner simply moves out of the marital home and the couple works out the details without courts or lawyers. This is a great option for those on the fence. It is for those, "Should I stay, or should I go?" people. This will enable you to see if you can afford two residences. It could bring clarity to the situation. If you are more miserable apart than you were together, you can easily get back together. It may enable you to retain financial perks of marriage, like tax benefits and health insurance. If this informal separation arrangement is working, you can keep it going. Parents can even work out informal custody arrangements to see what works best without paying for lawyers. You keep control over the situation. Any assets or debt acquired during an informal separation are likely considered marital property. If a divorce does happen, the conditions of the informal separation may be relevant. For example, if you leave and choose to spend no time with your kids, that may hurt your custody case should you get divorced.

2. LEGAL SEPARATION

Not allowed in all states, but if it is allowed, it typically involves a court order and contracts that spell out the terms of the agreement between the couple. While it does involve the court, I'm including it in this section because it does not generally involve litigation and a Judge controlling your life. Legal separation contracts include among other things, alimony, property, and childcare agreements. While legally separated, you can't remarry. Advantages of legal separation over divorce can include being able to keep health care (depending on the insurance) and other benefits like tax, military, and social security that terminate with divorce. Additionally, if the terms of the separation agreement are working and you decide to get divorced, you have already resolved a lot of the divorce issues. There may be less, or no litigation needed. But this option is not all flowers and sunshine. Here is why... A legally separated spouse still has the status of next of kin for legal or medical decisions. A separated spouse still has legal rights to the other spouse's property when that spouse dies. Hmmm... The separated spouse makes medical decisions and then gets the property rights should their spouse die. If I were on a ventilator, I would not want my separated spouse who benefits from my death deciding whether to pull the plug. Would you?

3. CONSCIOUS UNCOUPLING

Conscious Uncoupling is the brain child of Katherine Woodward Thompson, a marraige and family therapist. According to the website, https://www.consciousuncoupling.com, Conscious Uncoupling is, "A 5-Step process for how to end a romantic union in honorable, gracious and respectful ways; A step-by-step road map for how to break up in a way that does minimal damage to all involved; A clear guide for how separating couples can create new, cooperative life-affirming agreements and structures that set everyone up to win moving forward."

Having followed The Grateful Dead, I love this option!!! It is all spiritual and new age. The focus is on healing from the trauma of your broken marriage. According to Marianne Williamson, who approves of conscious uncoupling, it can enable you to turn your divorce into a "sacred journey from sorrow to peace." Since my divorce was hardly a sacred and healing journey, I'm jealous of Gwyneth Paltrow, and not just because she is younger, rich, and gorgeous; but also, because she consciously uncoupled. I presume that means she is not bitter and jaded.

I'm still not sure what conscious uncoupling means for division of property and child custody, but if both spouses are focusing on their spiritual path to healing, they probably won't be fighting over who gets to keep the antique dining room chairs. I think that both parties don't even have to agree for you to consciously uncouple. So, don't let a narcissist ex who hired a $500 an hour shark attorney rain on your spiritual journey. Check out Thompson's work, and try to get your spouse on board with Conscious Uncoupling by explaining the exorbitant cost of attorney fees for contentious divorces. Can't hurt!!!

4. MEDIATION

The divorcing couple works with a neutral mediator. The neutral mediator helps both sides agree on the issues related to their divorce. While the mediator does not have to be a lawyer, the mediator is supposed to be extremely knowledgeable about family law. The advantages of mediation are that the setting may be informal, and you won't have to deal with the court schedule. It can take months to get a court hearing on an issue.

While this option sounds good in theory, there are lots of potential pitfalls. I called people who have studied the conflicts of interest going on with divorce mediation and was met with expletives. These very nice people upon hearing the term "mediator" started screaming curse words and sounding like they were going to have a heart attack.

People have biases, and mediators are people. People who train mediators often have conflicts of interest and biases that influence the mediators they train. If you and or your ex also has an attorney, that by itself could create conflicts of interest.

The mediator could try to please an attorney they like by acting favorably towards his or her client. This is an especially fraught situation when the mediator consistently gets business from that attorney and wants to continue getting business from that attorney.

Will your mediator be truly neutral? Do you believe in the tooth fairy?

Mediations are private. While that might sound good in theory, it tends to benefit the spouse with the most skeletons in their closet. Additionally, if negotiations fail, it was a waste of money. Also, beware... If you get court-ordered into mediation or your mediator was trained by certain organizations, your mediation could be part of the family court players' money-making shenanigans.

On google, there are lots of sites extolling the benefits of divorce mediation. It's cheaper! Less contentious! Better for kids! etc. Maybe it is. But it appears that most of that information was written by people who make money from mediation.

While I'm wary of mediation, if you know of couples who had decent divorces, and did mediation, find out where they went. Anything is better than family court, so explore any option that exists and has a good reputation.

Wait...I take that last statement back. Water torture is probably worse than family court. And, I think Divorce Arbitration might be worse than family court too. My understanding is that Divorce Arbitration includes most of the hell of family court, but you have to pay the arbitrator who acts as a judge and I believe you can't appeal an arbitrator's outrageous decisions. Plus, just like with mediation, the potential for the arbitrator to have conflicts of interest is huge. A friend of mine with a wealthy ex who did arbitration got screwed so badly she asked the arbitrator about his relationship with opposing counsel. The arbitrator did not respond, but he did keep screwing her while charging a fortune. I think she should write to the arbitrator again with the direct question, "Did my ex pay you off?" Why beat around the bush?

5. COLLABORATIVE DIVORCE

It differs by state, but the basics are as follows; The Merriam-Webster first definition of the word Collaborate explains this option. It is, "to work jointly with others or together especially in an intellectual endeavor."

With Collaborative Divorce, each spouse hires an attorney trained in the collaborative divorce process. Each spouse meets alone with their attorney to present their facts and desired outcome. The spouses and their attorneys sign a collaborative divorce contract. According to that contract, the parties will try to "collaborate" to resolve divorce issues. But if the process fails, the collaborative lawyers can no longer represent the spouses. The collaborative lawyers will be disqualified.

The two attorneys and spouses meet in joint sessions. There may be several negotiation meetings. Other professionals such as financial experts are often brought into the process. If an agreement is reached, the attorneys can take the agreement to the court and a judge will typically approve it and incorporate it into a divorce decree.

The agreement can include a co-parenting schedule and child support. It can include a financial plan that works for both parties with the goal of protecting as much of the martial assets as possible.

Collaborative Divorce has many of the same advantages as mediation. You have more control than you do with litigation. You are not dealing with delays from court schedules. But it can get expensive and it is a gamble.

Both parties have to pay lawyers and if the process fails, I believe you will have paid money for nothing...(and lawyer chicks aren't free!)

On the plus side, there is no mediator and, hence, no need to worry about mediator bias. Also, with "collaborative divorce" the spouses are present for all negotiations. I can't even count the number of times I sat in the hall at the courthouse while my lawyers "negotiated" horrible deals and kept me in the dark about pretty much everything. I am not alone. Friends who have been through family court have complained about sitting in court halls while their lawyers negotiated disaster agreements that Master's then shoved down their throats.

6. THE MAZER METHOD

Having been a victim of the apparent scams, profiteering and child harming going on in family courts, I identified problems with the system, came up with solutions and founded The Mazer Method.

At The Mazer Method, facilitators guide the parties as they craft fair settlements and move forward through the divorce process and beyond. The facilitators are neutral and don't represent one or both of the parties. The settlements are win-win because the priorities of each party are taken into account. The focus is on making sure both parties are in a position to maintain a decent lifestyle, healthy and happy children and the ability to thrive after the divorce.

Instead of hourly rates, the parties pay a reasonable flat fee for a set number of sessions. One of our goals is saving you a fortune on your divorce and making sure we are not incentivized by hourly rates to drag it out.

Under The Mazer Method parents work with coaches to create custody calendars that take into account the schedules of everyone in the family. These custody arrangements are flexible and can easily be changed as circumstances change.

Upon request, we continue to work with parents on an as needed basis to help with or adjust custody schedules. We also help parents deal with custody emergencies that arise from unexpected events. For example, if you want to take your children to a funeral on your ex's custody time or your boss sends you on a business trip on what is supposed to be your custody time, we can facilitate those changes with your ex. If you use The Mazer Method for your divorce, however, chances are good that you won't hate your ex and you will be able to work out scheduling conflicts without us.

Upon request, we will provide continued support and services for helping you rebuild and start your new life.

This is only an overview. If you want more information on how The Mazer Method would work for your unique situation, visit our website at www.TheMazerMethod.com, email Reneemazer@gmail.com or call (484) 716-9619

LET'S BANG THIS INTO YOUR HEAD ONE LAST TIME

Why should you use one of these alternative methods? In case you already forgot...

"THE JUDICIARY IS AS CORRUPT AS HELL..."
    -Lou Dobbs, Fox Business Network's Lou Dobbs Tonight, May 18, 2020

"AMERICA HAS BEEN LOOKING AT AMERICA'S FAILURES...THE NATION-STATE, IT'S CRIMINAL JUSTICE SYSTEM, IT'S LEGAL SYSTEM COULD NOT GENERATE PROTECTION OF RIGHTS AND LIBERTIES."
    -Cornel West, CNN's Anderson Cooper 360 show, May 29, 2020[1]

1: Cornel West was a Harvard Professor. He is an incredible Philosopher, Author, and Activist

Renée may be coming to a venue near you! She is available for speaking engagements.

In order to get gigs doing seminars at Synagogues and other places with lots of lawyers, I feel compelled to add the following facts:

1. About 2/3 of lawyers are NOT problem drinkers.
2. All practicing lawyers have NOT committed suicide.
3. My brother, Ira, and close friend, Robin Rosenberg, are lawyers and I really like them.
4. I am an Ivy League Law School Graduate... and I passed the Bar.
5. Some of my favorite people were my fellow attorneys when I worked at the Environmental Protection Agency.
6. According to my Grandparents, I am a direct descendant of Leib Sarah (1730-1791), who was a Rabbi known for being a "hidden righteous" and Rabbi Levi Yitzchak of Berditchev (1740–1809). He was a beloved Chassidic leader who inspired hundreds of plays, stories, and poems. He was known as the advocate "Lawyer" who represented the Jewish people before the heavenly court.

If you have a problem with me speaking at your Synagogue, take it up with them.

Abrams, Richard Lee. "How Corrupt Judges Are Destroying Our Society." CityWatch Los Angeles, 30 July 2018, www.citywatchla.com/index.php/2016-01-01-13-17-00/los-angeles/15903-how-corrupt-judges-are-destroying-our-society.

Baer, Mark. "If Utilizing A Custody Evaluation, Do So With Your Eyes Wide Open." HuffPost, HuffPost, 7 Jan. 2018, www.huffpost.com/entry/if-utilizing-a-custody-evaluation-do-so-with-your_b_5a5256b6e4b0f9b24bf3186e.

"Bradley v. Fisher, 80 U.S. 335 (1871)." Justia Law, supreme.justia.com/cases/federal/us/80/335/.

Berens, Michael, and John Shiffman. "Teflon Robe: 6 Takeaways From Reuters' Investigation of Misconduct by U.S. Judges." U.S. News & World Report, U.S. News & World Report, 9 July 2020, www.usnews.com/news/top-news/articles/2020-07-09/teflon-robe-6-takeaways-from-reuters-investigation-of-misconduct-by-us-judges.

Cho, Jeena. "Can We Finally Talk About The Elephant In the Room? Mental Health Of Lawyers." Above the Law, Above the Law, 8 Feb. 2016, abovethelaw.com/2016/02/can-we-finally-talk-about-the-elephant-in-the-room.

ClipArt Source : <a title="Gavel Clipart Free" href="https://123clipartpng.com/images/clipart-298138.html">Gavel Clipart Free</a>

Cranney, Joseph. "South Carolina: The State Where Judges Rule Themselves in Secret." ProPublica, 6 June 2019, www.propublica.org/article/what-happens-when-judges-police-themselves-in-secret-not-much.

"The Depressed Lawyer." Psychology Today, Sussex Publishers, www.psychologytoday.com/us/blog/therapy-matters/201105/the-depressed-lawyer.

Dutton, Kevin. The Wisdom of Psychopaths. Arrow Books, 2013.

"Educating Oversight Agencies." Center for Judicial Excellence, 31 July 2019, centerforjudicialexcellence.org/cje-projects-initiatives/oversight-agencies/.

"Forbidden to Protect." Lundy Bancroft, lundybancroft.com/forbidden-to-protect/.

Gambacorta, David. "The Great Pennsylvania Government Porn Caper." Esquire, 11 Oct. 2017, www.esquire.com/news-politics/a42234/porngate-pennsylvania-kathleen-kane/.

"Getting Through Tough Financial Times." Common Reasons for Foreclosure - Getting Through Tough Financial Times - University of Illinois Extension, extension.illinois.edu/toughtimes/common_reasons_for_foreclosure.cfm.

Greenberg, Gary. "Inside the Battle to Define Mental Illness." Wired, Conde Nast, 27 Dec. 2010, www.wired.com/2010/12/ff_dsmv/.

HG.org. "HGexperts.com." HGExperts.com, www.hgexperts.com/expert-witness-articles/the-client-s-guide-to-law-firm-overbilling-25863.

"How to Use Our State Integrity Interactive to Find Solutions, 'Best Practices'." Center for Public Integrity, publicintegrity.org/state-politics/how-to-use-our-state-integrity-interactive-to-find-solutions-best-practices/.

"Legal Encyclopedia, Legal Forms, Law Books, & Software." Www.nolo.com, nolo.com/.

Marianne Williamson on "Real Time with Bill Maher." The Real Time With Bill Maher , season 17, episode 22, HBO, 2 Aug. 2019.

Liptak, Adam. "Judges Who Are Elected Like Politicians Tend to Act Like Them." The New York Times, The New York Times, 3 Oct. 2016, https://www.nytimes.com/2016/10/04/us/politics/judges-election-john-roberts.html?searchResultPosition=1.

"Olson, Elizabeth. "High Rate of Problem Drinking Reported Among Lawyers." The New York Times, The New York Times, 5 Feb. 2016, www.nytimes.com/2016/02/05/business/dealbook/high-rate-of-problem-drinking-reported-among-lawyers.html.

"Pennsylvania Gets F Grade in 2015 State Integrity Investigation." Center for Public Integrity, publicintegrity.org/accountability/pennsylvania-gets-f-grade-in-2015-state-integrity-investigation/.

Pinsky, Drew, on Bloomberg Television. Dr. Drew narrated the 2014 movie Divorce Corp. and did this related interview in a segment called "new docu "Divorce Corp" Explores Business & Corruption in Family Court System." This clip was on the website www.divorcecorp.com, but is no longer accessible.

Popper, Karl R. The Open Society and Its Enemies. Princeton University Press, 2013.

Sapien, Joaquin. "For New York Families in Custody Fights, a 'Black Hole' of Oversight." ProPublica, 7 Mar. 2017, www.propublica.org/article/for-new-york-families-in-custody-fights-a-black-hole-of-oversight.

Snow, Keith Harmon. The Worst Interests of the Child: the Trafficking of Children and Parents through U.S. Family Courts. Burning Sage, 2015.

"State Integrity 2015 Archives." Center for Public Integrity, publicintegrity.org/topics/state-politics/state-integrity-investigation/state-integrity-2015/.

"Stump v. Sparkman, 435 U.S. 349 (1978)." Justia Law, supreme.justia.com/cases/federal/us/435/349/.

Turkat, Ira. "Psychologist Recommendations in Custody Disputes Can Be Harmful, Even Fatal." American Journal of Family Law, 2018, iraturkat.com/turkat/wp-content/uploads/2018/05/AJFL_Spring18_Turkat.pdf.

Weiss, Debra Cassens. "The Legal Field Attracts Psychopaths, Author Says; Not That There Is Anything Wrong with That." ABA Journal, www.abajournal.com/news/article/the_legal_field_attracts_psychopaths_author_says_not_that_there_is_anything.

Zimbardo, Philip. 'Philip Zimbardo." TED, www.ted.com/speakers/philip_zimbardo

ACKNOWLEDGEMENTS

First and foremost, I need to thank the brave, brilliant and altruistic Saint Maura McInerney, Esq. She restored my faith in humanity after the family court took that away. Without her, I believe my son would not have survived custody court and I would not have been able to write this book. See, I don't hate all lawyers. Also in the Saint category are Amanda Rich and Patrice Lenowitz who both worked hard pro bono for the freedom of a child they had never met.

I had incredibly impressive people helping me get this book done. I searched the world for Josh Caso, the artist who did my illustrations for Not Too Scary Vocabulary and found him! Yay! He drew the amazing cartoons in this book and again blew me away with his talent.

I got unbelievably lucky when I found Jessica Benson, a college student at a 4th of July party. She had the exact expertise I needed to get this book put together. She did a fantastic job, was crazy talented, super creative and a joy to work with. Check out her work JessBens.com!

I can't thank Carl Mazer enough!!! He is the best of the best and he is also a phenomenal graphic designer who put his massive talent into this project. Love you so much!

The stars aligned when I found Deanna Bandlien and Julia Parrick who are so much fun to work with!! They are very skilled at the things I suck at and she have an artistic flair that is a perfect match with my work.

The gift from god Michael Schwartz is proof my dead relatives are out there pulling strings behind the scenes. I keep being amazed by how kind heart- ed and smart he is.

Words can't even express how important Augie Conte has been for keep- ing me motivated and hopeful. Don't know how I would have gotten through my divorce without him.

Catherine Shefski was a great addition to this project and possessed the organizational skills I lack (ie. The ability to put together a bibliography). The wonderful Johanna Markind and the incredible Doreen Ludwig also graced me with their stellar scholastic aptitude. I am also grateful to Doreen Ludwig for her brilliant books on family court and I highly recommend them!

My kids Zach Sage and Fletcher are awesome. I am super proud of both of you! Let's hope that since the hell unleashed on you by family court didn't kill you, it made you stronger. I want to acknowledge my mother, Toby Mazer, for ininspiring me to start a new career while old. My brother Ira Mazer, my sister-in-law Jill Mazer, and my new sister Sherry Sternthal were super supportive of this work and I love you all!

For getting me through my bleakest family court days and helping me with his brilliant strategies, Christopher Graziola deserves a big hug, a kiss and a gold medal. For generously giving resources to my writing, I am grateful to my magnanimous friends who were my angels, Jackie Harris, Rick Yellis and Wendy Mueller. Because you are awesome and let Jess and I work in your basement, thanks to the Phil and Marla Folz family! For being great friends and helping me through getting kicked out of my marital mansion on the lake, a big thanks to Honey Schwartz, Kirven Talone and Sara Grim. For holding me near and making my fears disappear, I am beyond grateful to Joe Mass. For his positive energy and beautiful spirit that got me through a lot of drama, I am thankful for Ed Johnston

For being my cheerleaders and/or helpers with this book, here's a shout out to Dave Giorgio, Brad Augunas, Jackie Mazer, Harrison Mazer, Rebecca Schlifer, Berel Sternthal, Sherill Gilman, Joanne and Kevin Joella, Sid L., Karen Schafer, Ann Marie, Eva Zouras, Izzy Miller, Danielle Schwartz, Tony Iaquinto, Robin Rosenberg, Barbara Lawson Zieger, Maier B. Yomin, John Katzman (best mentor ever!), Mike Leibowitz (for keeping me alive with his bagels), Jami Harrington, Susie Lautman, Carol Mihm, Beth Rosen, Susan Diambrosio, Joddi Woodin, and Valori Zaslow.

For my good friends and fellow survivors of family courts, I thank you for giving me the wisdom to write this book by opening my eyes to the depth and scope of the atrocities going on in the system. You are, and I hope I'm not forgetting anyone, Christian Stahl, Maureen Horesh, Steven Burda, Sandra and Sherlock at Strengthen Our Sisters, Stefanie Forte, Bernadette B., D.G., Armin Parhami, Miriam B., Elaine M., Catherine Campbell, Suzanne Yurk, Suzi P., Elizabeth DeCordova, Tina Steeple, Nicole Gross, Lizzie, Sara N., Jude D., and Sophie S.

WHO IS RENÉE?

Renée Mazer was the creator of comedy based word builders including the Award Winning critically acclaimed and top-selling Not Too Scary Vocabulary. She was an honors University of Pennsylvania Wharton graduate, Penn Law Alumni, Mensa Member, Award Winning attorney, founder of High Score, a test prep company and a guest on countless TV and Radio Shows including The Today Show. Then she spent years in the travesty that is family court in America. Her case became part of a play that exposes the human rights violations taking place in custody courts. Instead of getting voodoo dolls of the court players, she chose to use her experience for good by writing this book and warning the world, "Don't be like Renee, from family court, stay the frick away!!!"